MW01229501

Confessions

of a

Quilter's Slave

Norb Lauer

To David

[signature]

Printed in the United States of America

Published by Grizzly Gulch Publishing
An imprint of WingSpan Press

The WingSpan name, logo and colophon are the trademarks of WingSpan Publishing.

ISBN 978-1-59594-300-2

First edition 2009

Library of Congress Control Number 2009923673

Confessions of a Quilter's Slave is dedicated to the creative, hard working people in the quilting industry, the talented quilters who are its backbone, the unsung, mistreated and misguided spouses (such as myself) who have been unwittingly conscripted and most of all, naturally, to my wife Ann without whom none of this hoopla would have been necessary.

Table of Contents

Author's Note

This tale is based upon actual events and real people – well, to be truthful, I guess it would be more accurate to say it is occasionally based upon actual events and there is a smattering of individuals who vaguely represent existing persons. This vagueness is not being done to protect the innocent etc., but is primarily a result of two factors: one, I frequently mix reality with fictional remembrances of events (a habit shared with most renown historians and electable politicians) and two, I just have a really hard time remembering names. But no matter, now, let's first and finally discuss the title.

I must tell you that my original title was *I was a Quilter's Sex Slave – An Expose of an American Tragedy.* I thought the title was possibly humorous and some time ago I read that books with suggestive, lurid titles often sell really well regardless of the content so I figured, hey, why not? Well there were many reasons why not, starting with my wife's ardent dislike of the same. Plus I mistakenly gave copies of the book to several friends (my wife's, naturally); they were dead set against the title and insisted that no self-respecting quilter would pick up a book with such an onerous and deceiving title (deceiving? Not necessarily in my humble opinion). I disagreed, but, as might be expected...I lost.

Next – Slave? Come on. Isn't that a bit of an exaggeration? I'll let you, dear reader decide that. And let me know what you think. Really.

Finally, a brief profile of my wife, let's call her, "Ann". Ann is fiber artist, quilter, teacher and now quilt pattern designer, amongst many other talents, including accomplished hammered dulcimer player and flutist. Whatever she is doing, her attitude towards creativity, work or play can best be described as ... obsessive.

You'll notice at the end of each chapter, I've included a Quilter's Slave Hint for your information and, hopefully, use. It will be highlighted and identified with a "**QSH**".

But enough groundwork, it's time to step into the never-before-exposed world of the evil, mind and soul trafficking of a quilter's spouse/significant other (to be PC).

The Beginning

Idislike and am immediately suspicious of those oh-so-well-constructed stories that abide by a clear roadmap of plot and character development. Give me a story that starts somewhere in the chronological last third of the book and fitfully meanders in and out of flash-backs, foreshadowings and the present and whose characters are non-memorable and/or whose personality traits switch elusively on the froth of the writer's whim. I may not be able to understand the book nor appreciate its inhabitants, but I believe that I will be a better, more astute person for having tried.

So why then is my first chapter *The Beginning*? Well, the events that unfolded in this section really did not occur at the beginning, but, in my mind, I associate them with what I personally believe was the true starting point for me: the beginning of my downfall.

Quilters love to party, to gather together – an ageless herding or flocking instinct, I suppose. And they are gregarious: although individually they frequently are quiet, conservative, introspective people, put them together and the walls echo with loud conversations and giddy laughter. My wife, I believe I said we would call her Ann, was having a group of them over to our home. I don't recall the occasion and doubt if any of those that were present could bring it to mind. Suffice that it met the needs of the group; it involved quilting, conversation...and food.

Anyway, it seemed to me that it would be appropriate – no, necessary – to have some sort of meaningful theme or introduction to such an ostentatious a get-together. After further reflection, I decided that since quilters frequently banded together and often in huge groups at such events as quilting conferences and so forth that it was their right to have some meaningful message to kick off these occasions – something like *The Star Spangled Banner* represents at sporting events. So this was to be something quite important, far beyond the simple joining of friends and peers at our home. This was a project which I could turn my full attention to. And so I did.

There were numerous false starts and vacuous words before the final vision came to me. I knew it was right. I could feel it, hear it, sense it and see it.

The setting, for unknown reasons, is breaking morning by a mountain stream. It's dark with barely a hint of grayish light in the distance. The only sounds are the stream bubbling over stones and fallen trees. The ground fog is heavy and rises up to meet the lightening gray. Slowly a humming begins, next a quiet chorus of women's voices joins in and then the chorus grows louder and stronger until it drowns out the murmurs of the stream and the clatter of the awakening birds. As the darkness fades and the vapor continues to diffuse, golden shafts of light fall on scores of women seated at sewing machines on both sides of the stream, softly humming as they work.

(Okay, so it makes no sense; this is **my** story.)

Now the women begin to sing in loud, clear notes that meld with the beauty of the mountains and daybreak. They sing, *The Quilters' Anthem.* (To ensure that you get the full effect, the tune is roughly that of *Old Soldiers Never Die, They Just Fade Away* – a song devised many years ago when General MacArthur resigned. If you are too young to recall that, which I'm sure, most of you are, it's totally unimportant – just make up a tune…sorry I brought it up.)

The Quilters' Anthem

> *Old quilters never die,*
> *They just sew away.*
> *Lone Stars by night,*
> *Log Cabins by day.*

Paisley prints flash through their minds
As they try to sleep,
Counting endless bolts of cloth
Instead of counting sheep.

Old quilters never die,
They just sew away.
Learning just one more trick
Such as appliqué.

Sashing and binding with flying hands
While nestled in their studio.
Trying hard to fully puff
One simply great trapunto.

Old quilters never die,
They just sew away.

Piling fabrics to the sky,
Listen to their mournful cry,
"Just one more yard
Before I die!"

Old quilters never die,
They just sew away.

Well, I was quite pleased with my offering and was all set to hand it to Ann for her to present at the upcoming gathering when I began to grow uneasy: what if it was not handled properly with the full explanation it deserved and what if it was not sung with the right cadence and emphasis? There was only one solution. I needed to do it – the whole nine yards: presentation, explanation and singing.

There were, however, several problems with that scenario: first, outside of a brief nod to a few of the ladies when I had accompanied Ann, assisting her by dragging huge stacks of cloth in or out of quilt stores, I had not met most of them and, secondly and perhaps most importantly, I am famous...infamous, I suppose is more correct, as a terrible singer – oblivious of pitch and unable to carry the simplest tune.

Naturally, I put these self doubts aside and decided it would be no problem; I also decided it might be best if I made this my little surprise for Ann and her friends – no need to burden her with any anxieties.

So the day arrived, a wonderful spring day full of life and promise. The group initially gathered on our redwood deck for coffee and various types of cakes and gooey pastries and then was to move into my wife's studio for the more serious work to come. After all were seated and involved in pleasant conversation, I ambled out, gave my very best welcoming looks and words, then proceeded to tell Ann that I had something to present to her friends (probably soon to be ex-friends). She was surprised, uneasy and reluctant, but gave a weak grin and introduced me to the smiling women. I proceeded to describe the reasoning behind what I would be presenting, gave a vivid portrayal of the envisioned scene and then burst into song. Amazingly, at least from Ann's point of view I'm sure, they howled, clapped and were delighted and delightful. And there I was, unconsciously and innocently cast into a new career – Quilter's Slave.

QSH
Quilters tend to be voyeurs.

There are Other Joys Besides Quilting

Of course, Ann was not always exclusively involved with quilting. There were many times when she spread her creative wings to other endeavors. Off the top of my head I can't possibly sit down and name all of them, but a few do come readily to mind.

Basket weaving: piles of reeds lined our rear deck and insidiously spread into our utility room. Trips to the river for canoeing and camping resulted in the rear of our station wagon crammed with these unwieldy sticks that poked into the back of my neck as I drove to our favorite streams, leaving red welts of wood hickies for the world to wonder at. Sitting by the river, quiet, peaceful, nature-full, I watched Ann wet and twist and string these things into what I must admit were quite attractive baskets – not necessarily useful, but certainly attractive. Naturally, there was the problem of stuffing the finished baskets into the small cargo area along with the unused reeds, resulting in even more neck welts. Once home, the baskets needed to be stored until given to unsuspecting friends and relatives. The useable house area shrank.

Solar images: some sort of magic coating on fabric allowed the sun to create remarkable images on cloth. But, to get really exciting images, one needed giant piles of leaves, twigs, dried grass and flowers and on. Once created, the large sheets of nature's photography needed to be stored until given to the unsuspecting... and the house area continued to decrease.

Mannequins: for a brief time, Ann explored the world of creating mannequins for interior designers. These life sized stuffed people were made, given personalities and appropriately dressed to populate new home displays. There was even a newspaper article about two of them in which the reporter named them Lawrence and Laverne and they became instant celebrities. As an aside, the various mannequins resided in our home for a goodly amount of time before being exposed to the public. I must tell you, it is a startling experience to wander into a darkened living room and discern shadowy figures seated on your couch when you know the house is empty. And then there was even beyond life-sized; there was a giant Santa head that was over four feet with wavy white beard and all. Think about the available house space now.

There were many more projects – far too many to describe in this brief account. But what I considered to be the final blow was paper marbling. Our house had become even more crammed with huge tubs of unbelievably unpleasant glup and piles and piles of special paper that was later dipped and swooped and prodded in those glup vats to create what I must admit were extraordinarily beautiful designs. But that was it: I finally decided to put my spouseful foot down. No more...enough, I wanted our house back and I wrote a brief poem expressing my feelings to Ann and her friends when they gathered for another of those frightful events.

To Ann on Her Marbling Day

I've watched the quilts and spreads filling the rooms to the door.
And seen fourteen foot rolls of batting cross-stacked from ceiling to floor.

There's been basket weaving with miles and miles of wet, mold-covered reed
Accompanied by dozens of sticky paint jars that you assured me you need.

There've been dolls and giant mannequins and projects with soggy paper and such
And yards and yards of material that some just might think was really too much.

There also have been enormous piles of leaves, twigs and grass to create images in the sun.

Without any doubt, you have clearly had fun.

But now you're into this therapy of marbling all things

In huge vats of gooey, awful, slimy, shuddering rings.

But I don't mind, really, not too much at all,

But just once, I wish you'd do something that was...well... small.

I'm afraid this didn't quite stop her, but it did result in a modicum of compromise (or so I let myself believe).

<u>QSH</u>
Vats of gooey glup can sometimes be arousing.

Handy Man

Each of us is endowed with many talents: special things that we are good at – sometimes even excel in. Unfortunately, we also have a wide variety of those things that we are not so good at and often some stuff about which we are positively hopeless. I have always been totally useless and hopeless when it comes to doing those handy man jobs around the house – or anywhere for that matter – or really, anything that has to do with making things.

In the early days of high school, as I was learning more and more about both my abilities and limitations, I once ventured into the world of metal crafts: designing and creating neat pieces of handy metal objects and jewelry. I spent a whole semester industriously designing (actually, the designing phase was pretty decent and I enjoyed it) and then crafting the result. I had decided to make my mother a bracelet for her birthday – out of silver with some intricate patterns etched on it, abstract shapes cut out of the sides and the crowning finale consisting of a mounted, emerald colored stone set in the center. It took many, many tries and the passing of the semester, shaping and etching and cutting, and reshaping, re-etching and re-cutting, but it finally came down to the last week and all looked great.

I wouldn't say that the entire class was interested in seeing me complete the job, but it is fair to say that the majority was and, probably most of all, my teacher. They gathered around. I had finished the setting for the stone, probably for the tenth time; the bracelet itself was formed and polished and glistened in the muted sun rays that managed to permeate the dirt crusted windows. I was now ready to solder the setting to the bracelet. I carefully placed the flux next to the joint, lit the soldering tool and grinned proudly and confidently at the encouraging crowd that surrounded my work station. I guess I had smiled and glanced about just a little too long for when I heard mutterings and groans and looked down at my work, I saw a shimmering puddle of silver oozing along the work bench, the setting erect and drifting in the mild current of molten metal. I never gave my mother a birthday present that year. I never seriously ventured into the troublesome world of making things or remodeling things. I knew I was free.

But time came round as it always does.

"Dave finished building Kathy her sewing cabinet; it's really nice, plenty of drawers, just the right size... and it's on wheels. She can move it anywhere she likes...very easy. It's really nice."

"Dave is a very swell husband. She is a lucky woman," I replied, sucking on a gin-sodden olive and got 'the look" for my pleasant comment.

"Well, it would be fine, if just once we didn't have to hire someone to do all the work."

"It would," I agreed and then suddenly remembered I had something very important to do elsewhere.

But, I must admit, it bothered me. What was the big deal? I could nail a few boards together; I mean Dave was really a nice guy and good at construction type things, but surely no rocket scientist. Perhaps enough time had passed that my disposition and talents were now ready for another attempt into the world of building things. And I knew exactly what Ann wanted. We had recently talked about getting in touch with Dennis, our indentured carpenter, and telling him what was needed. There were two projects: a rack to hold quilts and fabric and a table for laying out the quilts, working on them, ironing them and who knows what all. "NO BIG DEAL," I smirked and muttered out loud. And what a surprise that will be for Ann, I continued the thought.

So I carefully began to lay out my plans with not a hint of my gracious intentions passing my lips. The two objects would be placed in the basement, where Ann was just beginning to plan and form a workroom/studio to enable her to do business with interior designers and custom long arm quilting etc. The basement, at this time, was essentially empty – you know – a basement: about eight feet high with duct work hanging down here and there and support columns erupting out of the cement every some distance. I measured off several areas and made my plans.

The rack would be eight feet tall and eight feet wide and four feet deep with three layers of shelving. Okay, no sweat, six plywood sheets, six square columns for vertical support and fifteen boards for horizontal support. Nail those suckers all together, put the plywood in place, nail the be-Jesus out of them and there's the rack.

The table would be twelve feet long and eight feet wide and would just fit in between some of those miserable support columns I mentioned. None of the other ladies had a twelve foot by eight foot table. I sneered. And this would be one solid table. A jump-up-and-down-on-it-if-it-pleased-you table – no rickety deal like an old ping pong table or whatever.

So it was time to bring it out in the open – at least part way.

"I'm going to build you a little something. No biggie, but I'd like you to stay out of the basement until I finish. Okay?" I announced over pre-dinner drinks.

I think it's fair to say that she was surprised. But I must admit that her initial look of incredulity quickly changed to one of panic. A look that said this could be the biggest disaster of our lives so far. I was hurt.

But I began anyway. I started with the rack, believing it might be the least challenging. I doubt that any of you would want to use my plans as a blueprint for at home quilting projects, so I'll avoid noting most of the details – the cutting (and re-cutting) of the boards when I forgot which of a series of lines represented my final measurement; the replacement of plastic garbage cans with actual wooden horses when the boards repeatedly slid off during the sawing; the difficulty of one person (one very inexperienced person) attempting to hold multiple boards in place while nailing them together (nails were my thing – screws never); the unbelievable complexity of placing the shelves on the ledges I had created without them smashing to the floor and so forth.

The day did come, however, when all was complete and I could stand back and admire the hard work of some weeks (yes, weeks – not days). It was good; I felt almost god-like having had a vision and creating something from nothing but knot-infested timber and shards of iron.

The rack did lean – I must admit. But it was solid: you could throw heavy bolts of fabric on the shelves – no problem. Smack the sides with hammer-like blows; it stood sturdy as a stone monolith. But it did lean. When facing this magnificent structure, if you cocked your head a good ten to fifteen degrees to the left, it was alright and I smiled happily; I knew Ann would like it – I mean we all do have some imperfections, don't we?

Now on to the really important project: the world's largest, strongest home quilting table. My plan seemed brilliant in its extraordinary simplicity. First, on top of sheets of plywood that were to be the actual tabletop, I would lay out the rectangular base board so, this time, all corners would be at exact right angles – no more head cocking. I'd join the four base boards together still using all nails, naturally, and a lot of them. Then I'd temporarily attach the top to the base boards. After that, I'd attach the legs, hefty 4 by 4s, and, voila, except for the final nailing of the top sheets of plywood and the cloth covering I planned for the tabletop, it was completed. All went perfectly: everything came together… and with enviable square corners. It was… wonderful. Now it was time to turn the table over, setting it on its legs to complete the finishing touches. Unfortunately, I saw that it was just too big for me to handle by myself so I decided it was time to let Ann see all I had done and lend a minor helping hand for the final stage.

It was with some obvious consternation that she followed me to the basement, my wide smile and statements of assurance aside. She stared at the rack for some time and then said, "It's very nice...but isn't it just a bit crooked?"

"Well, if you look very hard, I suppose you might say it's crooked...but if it is, and mind you, I say IF it is, it still will function perfectly...don't you think?"

She gave me a long look, smiled the warm smile that motivates me to do bizarre things like build racks and replied, "It's just great. Perfect. Exactly what I needed."

And, true to my innate shallowness, I beamed.

I guided her over to the table. "I'm afraid I need your help to kind of balance this as I turn it over. I think the two of us can do it. Okay?"

Ann walked around the table and poked at the legs sticking up into the air. "Sure...if we can. The table really will be perfect...it's so big. It will really save me a ton of time."

You guessed it, I rebeamed.

With some struggling, we managed to lift the table towards the ceiling. Holding it in place, I reviewed the situation to make sure we weren't in for trouble and observed one noteworthy thing. With the ceiling a scant eight feet tall, the table width at eight feet plus the legs at about three feet, there was no way we could raise the table and turn it right side up.

"I think we had better set it down," I said much more calmly then I felt.

We discussed the situation – why I'm not quite sure, and I assured Ann that I would figure out something – no big deal. She looked a lot less convinced than I would have liked to see, but she attempted to hide her doubts and smiled again at me and told me she was sure I would and it would be a fantastic table. I was not quite able to beam, but the instinct was still there.

After she was gone and I could hear her working in the bedroom studio above, I did the only intelligent thing a grown man can do in these circumstances: I strode over to the table...swore mightily and kicked it. My toe hurt.

This was a toughie. I had nailed and nailed and hammered and hammered the legs to the table and the table to the base. Sure glad I didn't use screws which I could have removed relatively easily. And even if I could remove the nails without destroying the wood and my fingers, then what do I do? After a brief time, there was a "Eureka" moment and I knew the problem was solved. I'd cut the table in half, set it upright, then using steel joints, NAIL the suckers all together again.

It worked. And the table became the talk of the quilting group. The cloth cover came down the sides and hid the steel joints and Ann swore to secrecy the debacle of the table raising. I had been confident she would maintain her promised silence, but I was sure I saw sly grins and finger pointing pass amongst the women when they viewed the table...perhaps it was just an overactive imagination on my part.

About a month after the table christening, Dave came over.

"Hear you completed quite the projects," he said as I hesitantly led him to the basement.

"Yea, but they aren't much. I know it's the kind of thing you do all the time," I answered as we entered the new studio.

"Son-of-a-bitch, but that is about the crookedest rack I ever saw," he grinned and shook his head from side to side.

"Well ... yea, it is slightly off," I replied and edged away towards the table.

Dave didn't move; he remained in front of the rack and continued to shake his head.

"I got to measure that; I'll bet it's a good ten to twenty degrees off. Damn. It's like the walls in one of those funny houses."

"Yeah. Well, I've wanted to fix it up, but Ann's got it in full use now." And she did, bolts and bags of fabric jammed all three shelves.

"Damn," Dave said and continued to shake his head.

"Well, here's the table. This has really worked out great. I understand Kathy wishes she had one." I grinned my one-upsmanship.

"No room in our basement, buddy-boy. Heard you had a mite of trouble with size and cut it in half to get it up. Damn, I never heard anything like that either."

And so it went: a step by step review of all that I had done with a minute examination of the reconstructed table. A few side remarks such as "There's more damn nails in this baby than the last house I built."

But eventually he left. Ann knew how painful that little encounter must have been and worked extra hard to let me know how much she appreciated and used the projects and the studio. I was somewhat mollified, but then and there decided this had definitely been my last building project – and to date, to everyone's relief, I've stuck to my word.

QSH
Unfinished, unsanded wood surfaces can give unwanted splinters in unusual places.

Starting a Quilt Pattern Design Business

In our culture, from the earliest memories of childhood, spider-web-like career paths guiding you to your future provide you with alternate lives you might achieve: follow this path – no that's a bad one; go this way – well, maybe not and so on.

Words of wisdom and encouragement frequently slam into your ears and fill your mind to overflowing: "Janet is so cute with the longest eyelashes and what a voice for one so young – I'll bet she'll be a great singer"; "Henry has this extraordinary gift of math: the other day he counted to 20 skipping every other number – I think he'll be a great architect or engineer." Or even worse, there are children who have no dreams or aspirations placed upon them, no thoughts of what they might become – only a tremendous void of desire, knowledge and potential.

Well, whatever. Ann never had the slightest inkling that she might someday become a quilt pattern designer and I certainly never would have dreamed that I might end up assisting her in such an endeavor.

Over a drink one evening after having moved to Helena, Montana to begin our new lives:

"I really want to keep on working with fabrics, specifically quilting," Ann said.

"As opposed to keep on truckin?" I queried.

"And I want to do my own things; no more taking orders from designers who take orders from over-demanding clients," she continued without notice of my question. "But it's difficult to make a living creating quilts; the demand is low and the marketing is difficult. To sell quilts, it's basically consigning them to quilt stores and/or counting on the internet, or it's becoming a well known personality and teaching and traveling a great deal, or it's being in the rarified rank of the few really great artists...which I am not."

"Well," said I, little realizing that I myself was about to embark on a life changing sequence of events, "what are some of the other elements involved in quilting?"

And so we talked about the world of quilting. In fact, we talked about it off and on for several days.

"I like the idea of patterns," Ann said. "It includes my creating an idea and method from scratch, working with fabrics and colors and has the elements of a real business...which you can be a big help in."

"Ahh...sure," I replied naively. And so it began – our own quilt pattern design business.

First came her workplace. Our new home was literally nestled among giant firs and ponderosa pines in the mountains above Helena, a beautiful and inspirational site in an area known as Grizzly Gulch; consequently, the name of our business became...oh, let's call it Grizzly Gulch Gallery. But there was no studio (not a word or even a thought to build racks or tables or anything by yours truly). A very large unfinished basement/garage combination offered possibilities. Plans were made, contractors contacted and soon things were rearranged and framing and dry walling began. At the end, we had a very small one car garage and a fairly large beginning of a studio.

The studio soon was filled with a 14 foot long arm quilting machine, a 12 foot table, several sewing machines, a desk and shelves, racks, boxes and bins crammed with fabrics and books and magazines. Naturally, there was a design wall.

Now to work. Four quilts/patterns emerged, one right after the other, *Mist in the Mountains* (an abstract mountain scene done in a bargello quilt-as-you-go technique using great batik fabrics), *Up Stream* (a realistic art quilt of a trout under water created with fused raw edge appliqué and batik fabrics),

Jubilation (an abstract art piece again done in the bargello quilt-as-you-go technique, using colorful/contrasting fabrics) and *Love That Print* (a geometric design featuring large prints and presented in four different sizes). We quickly found that the quilt creation was the very tip of the iceberg – now to be followed by detailed, comprehensive instructions, drawings, charts and patterns along with a colorful marketing cover. Then they all had to be edited, printed, copied, collated, and stuffed into clear plastic bags. Now all that remained was that they had to be sold.

We (yep, we) hit the trail of quilt stores in the areas surrounding Helena. For a state in the lower ten percentile of population, there appeared to me to be an amazing number of vigorous quilt stores. Several days a week for a couple of months, we toured the stores (naturally with our van loaded with patterns) and Ann was able to be a featured speaker in several get-togethers of quilt shop owners. The Bernina quilt store in Helena and its owner were especially helpful and offered good, solid advice.

For beginners, we did okay and, more importantly, were learning the business. What this pattern stuff was really all about: how quilt shops decide what to buy and where to buy it and what drives the quilter toward different types and styles of patterns. (I guess it can never be too early to try to know what you are doing – but that's just a thought.)

As an aside, it's nice to note that after being in business over three years and currently having a line of approximately fifty patterns, three of those first four patterns remain in the top half of our unit sales.

We didn't quite know it yet, but it was clearly time to expand our thinking. And a chance meeting of a prior (I was going to say old, but that would probably earn me a punch in the jaw) acquaintance of Ann's provided the direction to follow.

QSH
There are always new techniques to be explored.

Gone Camping

There's a sign on my front door...
Don't work here anymore.

In late fall we decided to go camping in northwestern Montana and then on to the Canadian Banff National Park. Naturally, we needed to stop at quilt shops along the way and show them our new patterns. And the van, as always, was laden with quilting stuff and patterns as well as our camping gear.

During the drive, Ann read in a magazine that a professional teacher and nationally known quilter (let's call her Jackie) who had owned a quilt shop in St. Louis which Ann frequented had recently moved to Eureka, Montana, a small town on the border between Canada and Montana. Since we would be driving through Eureka, Ann called; she learned her friend was on the road teaching, but would return before we would be passing through on our way back to Helena.

It was a great trip, even with the frequent and time consuming stops at quilt shops (my perception, naturally). Northwestern Montana was beautiful with teal green glacial lakes and rivers. The Banff National Park could only be called breathtaking – certainly, one of the most gorgeous and unique areas in the world.

On the way home, we stopped in Eureka and were able to contact Ann's friend, Jackie, who immediately invited us to her home. In addition to pleasant and interesting conversation with Jackie and her spouse, Jery, enriched by sips of wine, Jackie looked at Ann's patterns and suggested that if she really wanted to pursue the area of pattern design, she needed to get a booth in the national quilt trade shows; one is held in the spring of each year, somewhere in the northern half of the country and the major one is held in Houston every fall. It would be costly, risky and hard work – but no do shows, no do business of any substance. In addition to thousands of quilt shop owners attending, this was also where the national Catalog houses and Distributors reviewed what and from whom they would be purchasing for the following season.

It was clear: we had no choice. So that nice, pleasant little camping interlude set the stage for all that followed

QSH
Avoid giant red ant hills when positioning your tent – itchy welts in difficult to get at places can be most uncomfortable.

"...You Are Really Good With Computers"

In most fields of endeavor, it's called a setup; in the world of matrimony, it's called an everyday occurrence.

"Honey, you have had a lot of experience and I know you are really good with computers."

I heard the words and pondered for a short while. The world of brave knights fighting fire-spewing dragons and multi-headed creatures with slashing teeth was pretty much over, but still, a man wants to be a hero to his love, so, today, we express our heroic stature in whatever form we can.

"Well... sure," I muttered. The facts were when I was quite young I had been heavily involved with computers – except at that time, computers were overgrown calculators occupying rooms full of giant, humming, throbbing machines that gorged on cards with strange rectangular holes. I remained connected with computers afterward, but primarily as a user, not a doer and the latest era of unbelievable high speeds, huge storage capacities, internet connections, web sites and amazing graphics was something I had not kept up with.... nor did I want to.

"Great. When you get a chance, let's talk about a few things that I think I could use your help with," she replied smiling and rewarded my correct response with a peck on the cheek – having been quite sure of my answer long before she asked the question.

The list of a few things was long and forever growing. It included such elements as: a really nice, very attractive, easy to use and update website, eye popping brochures and pamphlets with wonderfully striking photos and graphics, diagrams and tables indicating detailed quilting steps, perfectly laid out sets of instructions, emailing provocative, educational and humorous newsletters to customers etc., etc., etc. Thus my new career as IT/Marketing Manager was launched.

Good websites are weird and exciting things: the ordinary person's portal to the world of virtual reality. For commercial applications, shoppers are expected to experience the items as if they were in a store. The actual senses of touch and smell aren't there – not yet anyway, but outstanding visuals and a dab of sound and motion can really do a job on your customer. Our website is not great. Ours is...adequate. But even adequate web sites are amazingly time consuming to create and then to maintain.

If you have ever done any website building or maintaining, you know that there is an endless array of uploading to get information to your site. And the real kicker is that once you've oh-so-carefully constructed your page, it appears significantly different on the monitor than you expected or wanted it to.

Colors are the banshee of all web marketing efforts, particularly for quilting where there are infinite values and hues that are important to accurately portray. Good luck. The color you see on your screen is not necessarily the color that the consumer will see. The color on the monitor is not necessarily the color that will actually print on your beloved brochure or pattern. And so on. You must learn to trick all of the evil genies that lurk in the monitors, slither down in the toners and ink jets or parade through the printers... and that takes TIME.

The fact is I had always considered myself a "big-picture" type guy: concepts, principles, perceptions, approximations – those kind of things – never very good at little details and the so-called nitty-gritty. Not sure how to spell something, should that be a period or a semi-colon? what was his name anyway? which computer program is best for that application? etc. – these are all things your assistant and/or secretary should and would know.

Suddenly I found myself immersed – perhaps drowning would be a more descriptive verb, in the tiniest detail of every aspect of our business. No task too small, no action too meaningless: the king of minutiae in the land of menial.

Take websites again: what about the spiders that creep and crawl around your website (an invasion of privacy if I ever heard of one)? Of course there are specific things you can do that MAY delight the foul little buggers and send them scurrying back to their masters, the enigmatic search engines to tell them that your site should be mentioned at the top of the list – or, again, maybe not.

There are even website invasions by hackers. One day we received a breathless call from a customer who had just revisited our web site to reorder some patterns.

"There are sexual groans and moans and whispered four letter words being recited over and over on your website and all your patterns have disappeared."

"That wasn't easy to do." The words left my mouth before I could stop them.

A pause. "No, I mean it. It's awful and I thought you should know about it."

"Thanks so much," I said, trying to recover from my obviously stupid statement. "I thought you were someone just joking."

It was true and it took our web site administrator two full days to fix the problem and set up new security blocks to ward off the endless number of crazies that apparently have nothing else to do with their lives.

Then there are pixels and dpis and jpgs and tiffs and god knows what else. If you don't understand these terms, how can you expect to produce any credible type of brochure involving pictures? And again there are colors; they are just impossible. There's the fundamental stages of CMYK or RGB and there are hue and saturation curves, distortions, blurs, filters, liquefying and on and on. Not that a novice such as I can even begin to master any of these things, but you are continually confronted with all those aspects and need to attempt to blunder along as best you can – a most unsettling and discouraging situation.

Of course, there's also record keeping and reporting: customers, products, sales, margins, bill paying, profit and loss statements... ad infinitum. And sales promotions, brochures, patterns, instructions and correspondence pile up. Proper final editing of all the marketing materials proves to be an apparently unobtainable achievement. In short, it's the day to day, moment to moment realities of operating a small business. And who needs that?

In any event, it was a totally different framework and mode of operation for me. Goes to prove: "Never too late to teach an old dog..."

QSH
X rated animations are impressive, but, in my mind, a huge misuse of our great technology.

Trade Shows are the Biggies

If it is now clear to everyone that our all important world revolves routinely and obediently around THE SUN, it soon became equally clear to us that THE QUILT TRADE SHOW is the center of existence for all businesses involved in any and all aspects of quilts and/or quilting.

I had, unfortunately, been involved in some trade shows in other businesses, but never fully in the day to day, hour to hour, minute to minute guts of this frankly horrid experience. But that was about to change.

Quilt trade shows for those of you who have not been intimately involved are both bizarre and amazing.

Although there are many show venues for quilting businesses, as mentioned earlier, there are two major trade shows, one in the spring which is held in one of a rotation of cities in the northern areas of the U.S. and one in the fall which is always held in Houston, Texas. At Houston, there are actually two events, the first is a trade show for quilt shop owners and the second is a festival for quilters. Other quilt festivals are held for quilters throughout the U.S. with the big one being held in the spring in Chicago.

Naturally attendance figures vary considerably by show, but participants in one of these quilt shop trade shows can be portrayed as follows: there are anywhere from 500 to 700 vendors selling to quilt shops; of these, approximately 250 to 350 are selling quilt patterns. About 2500 to 4000 quilt shop owners/employees visit these vendors in their booths. In other words, there's a lot of people and a lot of action.

Being a vendor for the first time is an almost unworldly experience. It begins walking into a cavernous, almost empty building with cement floors and distant cement block walls and that is several football fields in width and length. Glancing up, you see a ceiling looming dark and uninviting about thirty feet above with metal frames running this way and that. Booth spaces have been outlined on the floor and the aisles are beginning to be filled with massive wood crates on large iron wheels containing products, equipment and displays to be used in the booths. These huge, silent crates lurking in the darkened aisles remind you of the Trojan horse so deftly moved into the unsuspecting armed fortress.

Men and women are scurrying in seemingly random fashion. Orange fork lifts honk and bellow as they weave in and out and back and forth. It's confusion; it's unpleasant; packing material and debris are everywhere; it's ugly.

For two days, vendors work frantically and independently setting up their booth areas. Metal poles rise up to delineate the booth spaces; drapes and fixtures create walls. Products are displayed on racks, tables, hung from poles and attached to fabric curtains. A semblance of order begins to appear. The morning of the show opening, the vendors return to an area that has been magically transformed. Colorful carpets cover every inch of the floors; bright lights beam down upon artistic displays. It's like the wonder of a Christmas morning to a sleepy young child rubbing his eyes and staring at the magical, glittering tree.

Taking down the displays and booths is just as strange. In a matter of hours, the entire area is once again reduced to a barren wasteland, silently waiting for the rejuvenation process to begin all over again.

Our very first trade show was at the Spring International Quilt Market being held in Minneapolis that year and I'll discuss it in some detail as it pretty well hits the highlights of typical and memorable trade show experiences.

We had been in the quilt pattern business for less than six months and Ann had produced thirteen of what we considered to be stunning, artistic and unusual patterns. Our only feedback to date had come from a few nearby quilt stores in Montana and very nice and helpful evaluations by one of the major fabric firms. But we were excited and optimistic as is the right of the naïve and the innocent.

We had a contract for a booth (one-half size befitting our newness and product line – that's six foot deep and ten foot wide) and, again with the help of the major fabric company, had an excellent spot next to them. That's pretty much all we knew. We wanted to keep expenses to a minimum, so we decided we would drive to Minneapolis and would do some of the booth equipping ourselves, such as the carpet and lighting and we would book an inexpensive hotel.

We loaded the car: quilts, patterns, pattern holders, quilt racks, paper work, charge machines, rolled up carpet, track lighting, tools, brochures, clothing etc., etc. Oh, and yes, since we were going on to visit friends and family after the show, our faithful dog, let's call her, "Chutney", was wedged in among the stacks.

The trip from Helena to Minneapolis was fairly long, about 1200 miles. A trip that several years ago (that's all ...several) I would normally have done in one day. Aching hips and knees had recently made this distance unpleasant to impossible, so we planned a two-day trip. We are both ardent mountain people. Having lived in St. Louis, Missouri for way too many years where mountains are a thing of nonexistence, we were thrilled with our surroundings in Central Montana, but not quite so thrilled with Eastern Montana, North Dakota and Minnesota with its fairly flat, occasionally inspiring, never mountainous topography. So the trip seemed long with our highlight being passing through Fargo. But we arrived safely and just slightly the worse from the normal traumas of road travel.

QSH
Be wary of hitchhikers with lip rings or those toting sewing machines.

Trade Show: Minneapolis – Day 1

We had chosen our hotel for two reasons: 1) It was relatively inexpensive for a city hotel and 2) Really number 1 for us, they accepted dogs.

Since we needed to have a place for Chutney before we began the unloading ordeal, we went to the hotel first. Now, to be fair to me for having chosen this specific hotel, it was a national chain and is generally average to occasionally above average – but not this specific hotel. This one was located in what might euphemistically be called a run-down area of the city, pleasantly huddled among a bus station, pawn shop and liquor store. Our first reaction was to forget it and go find something else. This later became a clear lesson that you should always heed your first instincts. But we didn't. We were in too much of a hurry to start the unloading and knew it would take a fair amount of time to find another hotel downtown that would allow dogs. So we went to our room. It was absolutely horrible. We were directed down a long, dark corridor with no sign of other humans anywhere and the experience was as close to being in a dilapidated jail cell block as you could get without having been sentenced.

Once in the shabby room, I called the desk, told them how I felt and they reminded me that they only had certain rooms that allowed dogs. I told them that the dog was with us – we were not with her and we wanted some decent accommodations. After much ado, we were given another room, not a lot better, but at least it had a door leading directly to the parking lot and windows from which you could actually see the outside. We unpacked our clothes, said a fond and hoped it was not our final farewell to our beloved dog, and were on our way to the convention center.

Unloading was our first challenge. The nice attendant had us park our car at the furthest possible distance from our booth – it was uncanny how he managed to figure out the distances so quickly. We had no cart to load our large piles of possessions onto so there were many trips – many, many trips. I believe I have already mentioned that for the past year, I was having hip problems that were becoming more and more debilitating. So my leg dragging progress back and forth to the booth was reminiscent of Bois Karloff's mummy movies for those of you that may be old enough and foolish enough to have watched them. Well, finally we were unloaded and that's when the dismay set in. How in the world were all these quilts patterns, racks etc. going to fit into an area that was about the size of a small bathroom?

Undaunted, we began setting up the display table and laying out the booth. Hours passed, progress was non-evident, the convention hall lights flickered and a mechanical voice told us all to leave – tomorrow it would open again at 8 AM for everyone to finish the set up.

Weary, hungry and concerned for our dog, we headed for our hotel. Naturally, the first thing we did was to take her for a walk. It had not been dark long, so there were only a few bodies passed out along the curbs and huddled next to the crumbling brick buildings. Under the street light leading back into the hotel's parking lot, there were two lively young men handing out small packets of something in exchange for rolls of bills. I decided it was probably not a good idea to ask them what they were doing – my mother did not raise dummies. We left our disgruntled dog in the room and went out to eat. Actually, several blocks away there was an Italian restaurant that was pretty good. We ate, drank some wine, and returned to our room where we had some more wine from bottles that we had the foresight to bring with us. We talked about plans for the next day, read some and settled back for a spotty, but generally undisturbed night's sleep.

QSH
Not tonight sometimes makes sense.

Minneapolis – Day 2

Six feet by ten feet – close to grave size. How long can it take to stock, display, beautify, etc. an area that size? As you probably recall, we spent some hours the day before, unloading, playing handicapped beasts of burden and planning our next steps. The next steps occupied our entire day from 8 AM to 8 PM. A person could have easily and comfortably moved into a three bedroom, two story home in that period of time and ended the day lounging in their new quarters, smiling and sipping drinks and munching on French cheeses. Such was not our case.

What follows is a brief description of our booth efforts that lasted the entire day with the only "break" being about an hour interruption for Ann to present a Schoolhouse lecture of which I will provide highlights in the next chapter.

First, there's the matter of drapes. Booths must be draped per some prevalent, barbaric custom, similar to lining coffins with white, silky material. And the drapes must be pleasant, perfect fitting, pressed, pleated and ruffled ...whatever. I mean who cares? For days, quilt store owners and then quilters, crazed with pheromones dispensed by infinite bolts of fabrics and lines of tempting supplies and accessories, will stagger blank-eyed in and out of booths, collapse on chairs at any opportunity and watch unconcerned as smiling helpers swipe credit cards that are approaching newly extended limits. How important can drapes be? Very important, I was told.

Drapes need to be hung on metal framework generously provided by the convention center at an exorbitant rental cost. The poles lean and shudder at every touch and occasionally just collapse, sending fear and dismay among the surrounding booths. Something called sleeves need to be ruffled, just so, on the vertical poles and then ruffled again...and again.

Drapes finally hung, it's time to display the quilts – our raison d'etre, the beacons that draw a select few out of the thousands of passing lookers and buyers into our booth. "Love us," they cry. "Buy our patterns," they plead.

Quilts are different sizes; different colored quilts must be displayed next to each other in a complementary fashion; different styles of quilts must be considered. In summary, there is an infinite number of possible arrangements, none of which quite fit...it is, after all, a small, small space. Eventually, they were hung – not to Ann's complete satisfaction, but at some point, it became clear that compromise was necessary if we were to move ahead to the next steps within our remaining time.

Patterns then needed to be displayed; after all, selling patterns is the only source of income that will help defray the costs of operating a trade show booth. (Please note that I did not say cover the costs and provide a proper profit for the time, expense and effort.) The allotted time had almost elapsed when we finished. We smiled tiredly at each other, stepped out into the wide aisle to view our endeavors... basically, we were pleased.

The nice gentleman from the booth next to us (the major fabric company who had taken us under their wing) ambled over and stared at our booth with us.

"Well," he said, beaming his friendly smile, "there certainly is no wasted space."

He patted us on our shoulders, wished us good luck and sauntered off. This was not exactly the complimentary, "Oh, my god, how did you mange to do such a wonderful booth on your first time?" that we were hoping to hear. Tiredness enveloped us as we slumped out the rear exit toward our car which was barely visible in a far, dark corner of the lot.

QSH
Not tonight sometimes makes sense for several nights.

Schoolhouse

We were perhaps, if possible, even more unprepared for the Schoolhouse event than we were for the displaying of our booth. The Schoolhouses are series of lectures/demos given to quilt shop owners, managers and employees; they are scheduled throughout the day with approximately 20 different lecture/classes being conducted at any one time. These lectures are either fifteen minutes or thirty minutes long and attendance varies from packed audiences of 100 to 200 people down to "select" audiences of a half-a-dozen or so. We hoped we would be near the former, but had night-sweats over the possibility of the latter.

But first we had to get to the class room; that shouldn't be a huge problem. Wrong. The class rooms were on the third floor and at the far end of the huge convention center with our specific class room being at, naturally, the extreme outer bounds. As you may recall, we had neither carts nor even an omnipresent wheeled suitcase that dots the airports and are practically glued to the swollen hands of all earnest quilters. So we trudged up escalators, wandered down long, endless halls in peculiar number sequences, bent and swaying under stacks of quilts that we could barely see over. Occasionally, the quilts slipped to the floor and often helpful quilters aided us in the restacking.

With so many classes going on, everything must be timed perfectly so that the old class can exit, the new teacher enter and setup and the new group of students find their seats, all within five minutes between sessions. Amazingly, that part worked reasonably well.

The class room was packed. I had expected to help get the quilts there, assist in getting ready, then leave and come back at the end – possibly even stopping to lounge in a chair and sip coffee while watching with knowing amusement the other teachers and drafted helpers plodding their burdened paths to their class rendezvous; so, naturally, I was in my work clothes of jeans and a ragged T shirt. All at once, I found that I was passing out teaching notes, brochures and welcoming nice ladies and before I even quite realized that I was still there – no coffee, no lounging, no amusement – I was holding up quilts pointing to design elements Ann referred to and bantering with the class.

But, overall, it worked great. The attendees were responsive and enthusiastic. No cry of "tar and feather them and run them out of town." That gave us the motivation that we badly needed to finish the booth and look forward to opening day.

QSH
Staying after school with teacher can sometimes be rewarding.

Minneapolis – Night 2

We just wanted to go to bed, but our dog needed to be walked (I had wandered out of the convention center for about a half an hour around midday to take her out and make sure all was well) and we needed some food. Basically, we hadn't eaten the entire day. So after a close repeat of the previous night, we returned to the hotel, settled down in our dismal room, got out the wine, turned on the TV, which we don't have at home, to veg out and mindlessly and slowly sink into a deep and restful sleep to prepare us for the next day, the Grand Opening of the International Quilt Market.

We hadn't shut off the TV nor quite closed our eyes when the noise began. The area where they had finally placed us – the dog-allowed area – was at the rear of the hotel in a separate two story building with its own parking lot; the structure housed approximately forty rooms and up until tonight, as far as we could tell, only two rooms were occupied, ours and one other at the opposite end. So we had been pleased that, despite all the many other shortcomings, at least we were alone. Then engines roaring, horns blaring, headlights flashing on and off, cars began to arrive; it seemed very close to an invasion. Pushing aside the tattered blind, I peered suspiciously out the window. Autos were jamming into all the parking spots and, in many cases, just parking in the middle of the driveway. Loud voices, high laughter and exuberant screams were in all-time surround sound. Hotel doors banged; TVs and radios began to blast into the once silent night. Girls in strapless, white taffeta dresses paraded from car to car, room to room. Boys in black, white and tan tuxedos smacked each other in friendly banter and whistled and hooted at the passing opposite sex.

Well, we are not prudes, and have always considered ourselves to be friendly, fun loving, people oriented, just plain nice folks. But we did need to get some rest; tomorrow was a very big day for us. A day we had worked toward during the past four months, let alone considering the ordeal of the drive and setting up. The least we needed to do was to find out what was going on. So I made my first call to the front desk.

"There's a huge number of people moving into the rooms in our section."

"It's a hotel."

"I know it's a hotel, but it is pretty late at night and when I say a large number, I mean somewhere between and 100 to 200 people."

"Well, it is high school prom night, isn't it?"

"It is? Well what are we supposed to do? We really want to get some sleep."

"They'll quiet down. Don't worry. Have a good night."

He lied. The noise expanded exponentially. The teenage partiers were now going from room to room and banging on the doors, asking things such as "Is Clara in there? Who has the Wild Turkey?" Now I assume these are teenagers – it being a high school prom, but as we peeked out from behind the blinds, the boys seemed full sized, easily capable of sidling onto a professional football field the following Sunday and the girls were... let's just say voluptuous. I called again.

"This is nuts. You need to do something."

"What seems to be the problem?" a sleepy voice responded.

"The problem is they are yelling and screaming and pounding on doors...including ours."

"I won't let them in, if I were you."

"I don't intend to let them in. I'd like you to get someone over here to quiet them down."

"I could send the security guard."

"A great idea, and to think I thought you were stupid."

The phone slammed down.

In about five minutes, a voice rose above the din.

"Look kids, we had some complaints."

At this time we weren't looking through the grimy glass, but I was sure he was pointing to our room. After all, we were one of two rooms not rented for prom night.

"Get back to your rooms and keep it quiet." And he left.

We were quite surprised as we heard doors open and close, a few mutterings and then relative quiet. We pulled the covers up. It was now about 1 a.m.

Our room, although on the first floor of rooms, was on a second level. A deteriorating three foot wide concrete balcony ran in front of it along the length of the building; a rusted metal railing tottered along the edge – much more for appearances than safety.

It was a good five minutes before it all started again. Most of the deranged youths were now on this balcony. There was a great press of bodies, three to four deep, on the narrow walkway and I was sure the weakened slab would collapse and send bodies hurtling to the asphalt. Uncharitably, I thought that might not be such a bad thing. But the balcony miraculously held. Now it was the windows I worried about. The celebrating teens milled about and leaned against the outside walls and windows, apparently unaware or just plain unconcerned, that the sheets of thin glass were seriously bowing inward. It was reminiscent of a scene out of "*The Haunting of Hill House*", where the doors and walls buckled and swayed to the furious attack of the house's evil poltergeist. And they pounded on our door, continuing their never ending search for Clara or Barb or Billy or Wild Turkey.

Time passed; I called again.

"I want a guard stationed over here for the rest of the night."

"Maybe you'd be happier in some other hotel."

"I'm sure I'd be happier in any other hotel. But it's two in the morning and we're not going anywhere."

"Well, we put them out there so they wouldn't bother the people in the hotel. You shouldn't be there."

"That's the first thing you've said that I agree with, but no one told us about this. Now we need you to control this...and now."

"You have a dog. I just looked it up. That's where we put people with dogs, either there or in the abandoned wing. And...hmmm, I see here you didn't like that."

"I'm going to come up there and strangle you. Do you understand that? I want a guard here."

The phone went dead. About five minutes later, the guard returned. In an extra loud, deep voice, he said, "Kids, you get back to your rooms or you will be in real trouble. We've had some more complaints." In my mind, I saw him give a conspiratorial wink and a nod towards our room again. The quiet lasted almost ten minutes this time. I waited a while longer. The noise increased; the window bowed; the doors were pounded.

I called again.

"I want the manager."

"He's not here."

"Give me his home number."

"Are you nuts? He's sleeping."

The phone went dead.

We got out the wine. We were strong and determined; we could and would outlast them – after all, they were just high school punks. We were just starting to nod off as the light of the new day's sun filtered through the dirty gray blinds; it was finally still, the windows no longer shuddered; no shadows loomed outside our room. We had won. We had outlasted them. We grinned our victory and hugged. Suddenly, there was a pounding on the door.

"Hey, Jimmy, you in there? I need some of that Wild Turkey, man. Come on, man, open up."

We shrugged and stumbled out of bed to shower and dress – didn't want to be late for our big day.

QSH
Drinking and sex don't go together – especially if it's not you doing the drinking.

Minneapolis – First Trade Day...and Night

Now this was the real thing; what we had been planning and working for over the past four months. The day started less than well. For this opening day, the shuttles to the convention center were full – loaded before they ever got to our hotel. We were going to be late. A chill wind stirred the gray air and swirled dust and papers around the car-crammed street. In spite of the coolness, I was sweating. I spoke to the man at the front desk.

"We need a ride to the convention center."

"The shuttle will pick you up out front."

"The shuttles are full."

"I'm sure there'll be one with space on it shortly."

"We're exhibitors; we need to be there."

"I understand."

The phone rang. He grabbed it, turned his back and hustled out of sight. I went to find a taxi. It took a while with some battling for position with other aroused convention goers, but we managed to race into our booth with about ten minutes to spare before opening. We made last minute arrangements and stood back to admire our presentation. A bell rang; a disembodied voice obviously trying to smile through the sound system told all that the International Quilt Market was now open.

It was a good forty-five minutes before one person stopped at our booth.

But then they came. Crowds...no, gangs might be a better description, crammed into our small space until we frequently found ourselves out in the aisle, peering in at the gathering. Many of the people stopping had been at our Schoolhouse the previous day and couldn't say enough about how much they had enjoyed the session and loved the patterns and quilts.

And they bought...and bought. This was getting to be fun. I was beginning to enjoy the experience and forget about the few minor problems and inconveniences we had encountered along the way. I mean, after all, it can't just be a slam-dunk or everyone would be doing it. Towards the end of the first day when there was a slight lull in chirpy buyers, my complacency was once again shattered.

"I wonder where they are," Ann said in a stage whisper.

"Who?" I asked, still grinning in my gross ignorance.

"The distributors and catalog companies. You remember; we need to establish relationships with as many of them as we can. You're the one who said that more patterns are sold through them than directly to the stores."

"Oh, those distributors and catalog companies."

"Not one has been by yet… or worse still, maybe they walked by, stole a glance and kept right on going. There must be about 300 other pattern companies here – many of them have been coming for years." She was clearly over the exuberance of the busy first day and …now, so was I.

The first day ended and we returned to the hotel, walked our dog and went out for a meal with our friend and mentor, Jackie. Over dinner, she insisted that we had had an outstanding day, particularly for our first market and that the distributors and catalog folks often didn't come around until the 2nd or 3rd day of the show. In a short time, the conversation, drinks and meal had us commencing to feel pretty darn good about the show and ourselves. A good night of rest and we would be smoking tomorrow.

When we returned to the hotel room to walk our dog before dinner, we ran into the head night security guard. He somehow knew who we were and made a great effort to apologize for the previous night, informing us that he had been off duty for the night or that whole mess never would have happened. He assured us that all the prommers were gone, and whispered conspiratorially that he was glad of it. Waving and smiling, we had gone off to dinner feeling confident of a relaxing and sleep filled night ahead of us.

Hand in hand, we strolled into the back parking lot and our section of the hotel. No young boys and girls hooting, screaming and revving engines. No tuxes and shiny dresses and expensive hairdos greeted us. No. Instead middle-aged men, many of them balding, were staggering up the stairs carrying heavy coolers obviously filled with beer. Several also not-so-young women leaned provocatively in open doorways. From one room, the sighs, moans and groans of an XXX rated movie blared into the salacious night.

At this point, I believe that some of you may have started shaking your head and insisting that my imagination had indeed captured the moment and moved well out of the realm of reality. I assure you this was not so.

Naturally, the series of phone calls began.

"There's some kind of sex orgy going on back here." I muttered to the same disinterested voice of the previous night.

"Why do you feel a need to tell me that, sir?" He inquired with a definite hint of malice.

"The rooms all around us are filled with middle-aged men and ...let me be kind, ladies. They are going from room to room, singing, shouting and the TVs are screaming out orgasms."

"Oh... you must be referring to the bachelor party. There is quite a group of them."

"Oh, golly, yes, I guess it must be the bachelor party...well, now that we know what it is, what are you going to do to quiet it down? With two sleepless nights in a row, I could easily become murderous."

"I suppose reminding you that this is a hotel and open to the public and public functions will do no good?"

"Send the security guard down here before you need one up there."

"Are you threatening me?"

"Yes." And the phone went dead once again.

I'll not go into the details. There were numerous iterations of noise, calls and security guard visits. By well after 1 a.m., only a few doors were slamming, an occasional refrain of "He's getting married in the morning..." wafted into the late spring night and periodic canned squeals of passion ricocheted off the cracked, cement walls...a decent enough night for the likes of us. The light of dawn crept into the room through the same dirty shades and we staggered red eyed and weary into the shower, anticipating many shots of espresso before the show opened.

QSH
XXX movies are generally a turnoff –
unless, of course, you are making them.

"Wow, Quilters Come Loaded"

Well, what kind of comment is that?" Ann queried indignantly.

"No offense...really, but just look around."

We were perched on a chrome railing quickly sucking down early morning espressos before personing (please note the PC) our trade show booth. From our vantage point we could watch the shuttle buses disgorge group after group of exhibitors and quilt shop owners.

The exhibitors scurried off to their booths while the quilt shop owners found places to sit or to lean and study their buying guides and brochures with great fervor. In common...and almost in step, they pulled and yanked huge suitcases on wheels (who was that genius that put wheels on suitcases thus allowing people to carry extraordinary amounts of increasingly unnecessary stuff wherever they go?) while at the same time holding a death grip on one or more cloth bags already overflowing with magazines, brochures, fabrics and who knows what.

This would not be the only time we would observe this phenomenon. It was everywhere that quilters were. In the elevators of the hotels and convention centers a smiling group would press through the narrow opening and then jam against each other and the walls, suitcases and bags all smashed together, the bursting zippers silently protesting the continual overcrowded conditions. Often, the elevator door would open and close, open and close until finally a safety bell would ring and herald the overweight/overcrowded situation and someone would sheepishly clamber out and allow the up and down transit to continue.

Escalators were less claustrophobic, but from a distance the vision crudely reminded us of ants carrying amazing amounts of something to or from mysterious terminuses.

At the Quilt Festivals, quilters would replace the shop owners and they too would be loaded with the ubiquitous suitcases and parcels... possibly even more than those yanked about by the shop owners and exhibitors; often, they also had the additional burden of dragging a sewing machine off to classes.

For our part, for years, I had stubbornly refused to join the world of suitcases with wheels; I mean...just carry the stuff...what is the big deal? That was until we suffered through our first trade show. As I mentioned earlier, we really struggled with the initial unloading, but the impossibly long and unwieldy trips to and from Ann's Schoolhouse appearance was the final blow.

To elaborate more on that unforgettable event, the room for her presentation was at the extreme end of the third level of the convention center; our booth was on the other extreme end of the first floor. Sure there were escalators and elevators to get you to the top level. None in a straight forward fashion, of course. Take escalator 1 to area A then elevator Z to area 10 etc., etc. During a rare moment of good judgment, we actually managed to leave an extra large allotment of time to get to the room and set up – everything had to function smoothly and quickly once the room became ours.

As Ann was giving two Schoolhouse lectures back to back, it was clear to her...never had been to me that almost every quilt we had brought needed to be at the Schoolhouses. In addition to the fact that we had just completed hanging the last of the quilts and now had to take them all down, the number and weight of them was ...well, let's just say unimaginable, at least to me. So we piled and bagged and staggered on our way, basically unable to see without making a Herculean effort at balancing and peeking over and/or around the folded treasures.

Naturally, along the way, we managed to get lost and found ourselves in Corridor AAZZ instead of BBYY or whatever. The piles were continually slipping and sliding and occasionally slithered all the way to the floor. When we stopped...which was a lot more frequently then we wanted to, we got the opportunity to see the amused and sometimes astounded faces following our progress or lack thereof. Near the end of our journey, one man left the crowd of those watching our plight and offered us a four wheeled truck that he had been using and told us where to return it. Not to exaggerate, but he probably saved if not our lives, at least our souls.

Returning from my reverie, still leaning on the chrome rail sipping the last draft of coffee I said, "You know, I'm glad we aren't like that." Ann looked at me, a brief look of puzzlement crossing her pretty face, not sure whether I was kidding or had merely lost my mind.

"Me too," she replied without a hint of her decision regarding my condition.

Before we took down our booth, I had been able to purchase the first two of many suitcases on wheels. We now probably own more suitcases on wheels than your normal luggage store has in stock...so much for principle.

<u>QSH</u>
The clanking of steel wheels is often said to be erotic. (Or did that have something to do with trains?)

Minneapolis - The Final Days

The second day, Ann decided to get to the show before it opened so that she could stroll the aisles to see the other vendors' booths while I stayed back to walk our faithful and fast growing churlish-from-lack-of-activity dog. The day was sunny with the proverbial blue sky and pleasant spring breeze; I discovered a nice quiet park a few blocks away. Life was not so bad.

After returning Chutney to the room, giving her a few pats and words of encouragement which she accepted with a sigh and a clear look of disdain, I went down to wait for the shuttle bus. It came within three minutes. I walked down the aisle to find one of the few remaining seats and was greeted with pleasant smiles from the sea of ladies who looked up from their convention programs.

When I arrived at our booth, Ann greeted me with a giggle and immediately went into her story of her activities of the morning.

"The bus was out front of the hotel and I got on and started looking thorough quilting magazines," she began.

"That's new," I encouraged her.

"I had noticed that most of the women had a red scarf or a red something that they wore on their wrist, but I didn't think much about it. Anyway, after a few minutes, a woman boarded the bus and asked everyone to count out...you know, one, two, three and so on."

"Four comes next," I suggested helpfully.

Ann continued to ignore me and went on, "She got to me – I was number twenty-three – and gave me a puzzled stare."

"Maybe, you miscounted," I suggested.

An eye roll and she continued, "It turns out they were a church tour group, headed out of town to God knows where. I guess I could be someplace shortly, snapping pictures of cathedrals. I got off the bus pretty embarrassed. There were some more ladies standing there waiting to catch the right bus to the convention center and they greeted me with some smiles and laughter. Said, they had almost gotten on that bus themselves."

"Well, glad you made it. Would have hated doing this myself. And what's wrong with taking pictures of cathedrals?" I queried.

"Never mind," she answered and busied herself straightening quilts.

The day went great again; this time we were busy right from the opening with groups of "be-backs" who had taken our brochure with them to decide what to buy. Slightly tired, but still highly motivated, we spread out quilts, gave pattern highlights and took orders; time passed quickly. But a few wrinkles remained.

"I can't go to the bathroom," Ann whispered in the late afternoon.

"And why is that," I asked genuinely concerned.

"They may come."

"They?"

"Yes, you know the distributors and catalog people. They should have been here by now. Not a one has been by yet."

"You don't think I could handle them until you get back," I asked with a touch of pique in my voice.

She hesitated before replying, "No."

So she went to the booth next to ours to query Jackie, who, as a long time top pattern designer, well known teacher and highly respected member of the quilting industry, would know what was going on.

She came back smiling, said she was off to the rest room and quickly disappeared around the corner. When she returned, she explained that no major distributor or catalog house had been to Jackie's booth either and that Jackie had spied several of them in booths a good distance from ours. It looked like it would happen tomorrow.

The remainder of the day continued well, slackening off as the show drew near its daily closing.

We thoroughly enjoyed our first uneventful night, listening to some nice music on the radio and actually getting a good night's rest. Ann once again went in early to tour the remaining booths before the show opened and I walked our dog again through the green park with the small stream under bright blue skies and a mild breeze – all in all, a great start for the last day.

<u>QSH</u>
Learning when to wait can be a real virtue.

Goddess Speak

All businesses and industries have a hierarchy of some sort with specific companies and/or individuals confidently straddling the top of the ladder like the Colossuses they are. The Quilting Industry and specifically the quilt pattern segment is no exception. Several large Fabric Companies set the trends and process that sends millions of fabric bolts from foreign factories surging across the U.S. to the Distributors to the Quilt Stores and finally to the 20 million Quilters who huddle behind sewing machines amid piles of fabric and stacks of patterns. There is one Distributor from whom the majority of quilt stores buy their patterns and accessories and one Consumer Catalog/Website that individual quilters treat as their bible of worthwhile notions, supplies, patterns and kits. You do not really exist as a Pattern Design firm...or really even as an accepted individual in the quilting business, unless your products are carried by at least these two firms.

The morning passed and we continued to be very busy, mostly filling orders from the final day "be-backs" and lunch time came and went and the crowds in the aisles noticeably thinned.

"They must have looked in and walked by. We should have been paying more attention. I've been squinting at badges as often as I could, but the printing is so small," Ann said, tiredness and disappointment tugging her normally smiling, pleasant face into grim lines of anticipated defeat.

"Well, sure, we could have told all our customers that we were too busy to fill their orders and we would particularly appreciate it if they would stop blocking our booth," I answered. No grin from her – sometimes funny falls flat.

"Why don't you go ask Jackie again if they've been to her booth?" I went on, trying to redeem our lost camaraderie.

She did and came back shortly. She was almost jumping. "They're a few booths away. Since I don't know them, Jackie is going to give me a sign when they are in her booth. Hurry up; we need to do a lot of rearranging."

I had the good sense not to mention that we had been continually rearranging every time a customer left but, instead, silently and smoothly moved some quilts and patterns back and forth a number of times to indicate my undying interest and attention to detail.

Jackie's hand fluttered around the edge of the booth; the moment was almost nigh.

"I wish I had gone to the bathroom again," Ann murmured out of the side of her mouth while smiling into the almost empty aisle.

The air seemed to shift imperceptivity and three women appeared in front of our tiny booth.

One woman, clearly in charge, was accompanied by what seemed to be one assistant and one minion. Heads thrust forward like chickens on the way to the chopping block, Ann and I both strained to read their badges. Two of the badges had turned around and showed only blank whiteness. By a fortunate twist and swirl, the badge of the lady in charge faced forward. It was our long awaited Catalog Company and we could even read her name... let's call her, Carol.

The three barely acknowledged our presence, but walked up and down in front of the quilts, picked patterns out of the displays and glanced through them.

Carol conducted herself as she should: she was to our reckoning a Goddess who had decided to descend to earth and permit her presence to be seen by a few privileged mortals.

She spoke very quietly to her assistant who in turn spoke somewhat louder, but still in a hushed whisper, to the minion who nodded and shook her head while silently scribbling notes into a small purple notebook. And we knew and accepted this for what it clearly was: to our ears, it was *Goddess Speak*, far beyond our everyday mortal capabilities for hearing and comprehending. The undecipherable conversations and frantic jotting went on for what seemed a very long time as our smiles lay frozen on our faces like smears of icing from yesterday's birthday cake.

The Goddess approached. The intangible mutterings transformed into a pleasant, warm voice and the distant divinity into a smiling, charming lady who introduced herself and her companions. They spoke with Ann and I heard words like "very attractive and unusual." Suddenly, they were pointing at specific quilts. Ann was grinning and nodding and then, as quickly as they had appeared, they were back in the aisle on their way to the next and the next and the next booth.

"They are going to take three of our quilts to evaluate and photograph," she said squeezing me, obviously on the verge of a long coming breakdown. Among the quilt pattern designers, it was considered a true honor to have any of your patterns selected by THEM and something that probably never happened to most of the design companies... and it was our first show. We were both unbelievably excited.

Ann stuck her head around the corner, and Jackie joined us. "They took three of our quilts," Ann said before Jackie had even stopped walking.

"That's just great," Jackie said. "I told you you'd do well." And they hugged. Later we found out that THEY had taken three of Jackie's as well, but she had been far too busy giving us her genuine encouragement and acknowledgement of a job well done to mention it at that time.

After Jackie left, we stared up the long aisle and saw the threesome disappear into another booth.

"I wonder if they ever look back and see the "chosen ones" holding hands, hugging and dancing around ...or watch the unaccepted slouch back among their unwanted wares?" The question hung in the air unanswered.

QSH
Sex and success go hand in hand – both are often elusive and just out of reach. (Phrase stolen from stale fortune cookie)

Pitfalls Along the Way

Although each trade show has its own personality, they all have little challenges similar to those we ran across in our first show in Minneapolis. But there were some other pitfalls we encountered later that further added to our character building.

Naturally, it's not practical to drive to all shows; distance and time frequently require flying and, consequently, a whole new set of difficulties confront you.

To begin with, you need some type of shipping containers. While the concept is self-evident, the solution is not. We searched shipping and handling catalogs and visited hardware stores and big-box stores and had many non-illuminating communications on the subject with clerks and internet marketers. Of course, the seasoned and larger show vendors have it all worked out and often have the large wood crates loaded with their products and display materials that I mentioned in an earlier chapter; that was far too much for us newcomers. We finally settled on two 48" long, 24" wide, 20" deep plastic crates that "can withstand any amount of rough handling," per the hardware store clerk.

And there was our track lighting to deal with; we needed special boxes to hold the tracks, poles and attachments that would enable us to hang them across the booth and naturally the length was a non standard size.

Next we had to find a shipper. Trade shows appoint a designated shipper – you don't have to use them, but life should be easier and we wanted easy. Obstacles began to crop up as soon I attempted to book the freight carrier. As our studio is on a dirt road in the mountains, we would have to get the freight to them either by taking it to their depot in Butte, about seventy miles away, or via a series of phone calls arrange to meet their truck at some place in Helena and load it there. They went on to say that it would really help if the entire shipment was plastic wrapped on a pallet... Right.

The shipment day (over two weeks in advance of the scheduled set up day) arrived long before we thought we could be ready, but somehow we were. We needed to load the crates, boxes and cartons in our van and then haul them into town to meet the truck at a free standing cement truck dock at a location vaguely and confusingly described to me – no address. Since we had consolidated many boxes into the two plastic crates, they were slightly heavy, about 130 pounds each, and very bulky and the two of us had quite the struggle to get them up and in the van. As usual, the van was crammed top to bottom, side to side.

We were all set. Well almost. We jumped in our seats and I attempted to start the car. The battery was dead. You've got the picture, unload the van, load everything into our other, older and even more decrepit 300,000 + miles van and then we were off.

We were now running late and I had no means of contacting the driver. We bounced down the rutted dirt road, anticipating the rear end to fall off from the extra weight that strained the worn and rusted parts. Still in one piece, we arrived where I thought the meeting location was, but no truck. With desperation building, we drove around the surrounding blocks and finally spied the truck half hidden behind some abandoned trailers.

"I was just getting ready to leave," the driver grunted none-too-friendly. I returned the none-too-friendly grunt as we all walked to the rear of the van. He shook his head. "No pallet? How do you expect to get the stuff in the truck?"

"Lift it?" I queried.

"Not my job," he said as he spit into the dust and then nudged the moistened dust ball back and forth with the toe of his boot.

The end result was that after the driver sadistically watched us struggle to raise one of the crates to the tractor's bed, he started chuckling and then nicely pitched in to help. Like parents at their child's first group camping experience, we watched with mixed feelings of sadness and relief as the truck skimmed out of sight around the corner; our prized goods were on the way.

When we arrived for the set up at the convention hall in Houston, the shipment was sitting on a pallet in the middle of our booth, waiting for us. We did the old collective sigh-of-relief thing and then looked more closely at our things. Both plastic crates were broken (apparently they had been subjected to beyond rough handling) and edges of indiscernible things were sticking out. The box with the light fixtures was twisted and bent. The paper cartons all had gaping holes in their sides. To our credit, we did not moan nor cry.

Actually, amazing as it might seem, certainly it was amazing to us, nothing was broken, nothing torn, nothing damaged, but we clearly had a lot of work to do in the future to get the whole shipment process worked out – and eventually we did.

And, as we put more shows behind us, another factor became evident: we didn't have the foggiest notion of which new patterns would be out and out winners and which would be losers. We knew our favorites and our least favorites, but our ranking seldom matched that of the buyers. In speaking to other pattern designers, they had exactly the same experiences: frequently, the "newly developed, best pattern the world has ever seen" was accepted as okay and the "humdrum" was pulled off the shelves.

Finally, there's always the tremendous problem of scheduling. Every type of vendor constantly needs NEW products – that's the world we all created – that's the world we all live in. In a way, it all starts with the fabric companies; they introduce the new fabrics and the pattern designers use those new fabrics in new patterns and the quilters, quilt shops, distributors and catalog companies decide whether to buy them.

Most fabrics are manufactured overseas and most of the time, every one is playing the old beat-the-clock trick as the bolts of fabric always seem to be delayed in their arrival for just about every reason you could imagine. Once the fabrics arrive, everyone runs around like the over zealous hamster on a wheel. For the pattern designers, they must now convert the pattern to a quilt and hope it works out the way they thought it would. Most of the time, they have already tested the pattern using other fabrics and/or computer generated images, but you are never quite sure what it will look like until you see the finished quilt with the actual fabrics. Ann, as do most of the other pattern designers, fortunately has help at this stage as several very accommodating and talented local women pitch in and construct the quilts with the new fabrics; they do a great job in an extremely short time. Then the final photos need to be taken, covers to be printed, review of instructions and patterns to be prepared for sale. Who said life was easy?

When this stage arrives, I must admit I'm on the verge of testy and a typical comment of mine during a conversation with my over enthusiastic spouse might be, "Shhhh, don't ...please...do not even say the word, quilt."

QSH
Stress often hinders performance.

Quilting: A Cottage Industry?

Some sized cottage: the quilting industry is big (that's technical jargon in case you outsiders didn't understand). Of course, quoting numbers and facts about any industry is like telling someone your wife's age and weight. Chances are you will not get it right and, if you do, you'll be soundly remonstrated. _

But, I'll give it a shot. In the U.S., there are somewhere around 20 to 25 MILLION quilters who generate about 3 to 4 BILLION dollars of business per year. I realize that's a fair sized range, but good numbers are hard to come by – ask the U.S. Census takers.

Let's take a quick tour of the makeup of the quilting industry.

Positioned firmly at the top of the business pyramid are the Quilters. But there are quilters and there are quilters. There are beginning quilters, experienced quilters, and intermediate quilters. There are young quilters, middle aged quilters and older quilters; female quilters and male quilters. There are hand stitching quilters, machine quilters and long arm quilters. There are quilt artists, quilt professionals, quilt hobbyists, family quilters, traditional quilters, contemporary quilters, landscape quilters, pictorial quilters and geometric quilters as well as original design quilters, pattern devoted quilters and group quilters. And there are quilt markets, quilt festivals, quilt shows, quilt exhibitions, indoor shows and outdoor shows. There are quilting groups, quilting guilds, quilting retreats and quilting cruises. And there are fabric designers, quilting instructors, computer quilt designers, and quilt pattern designers. And this just highlights some of the categories of quilters and quilting – it makes my head hurt and I just don't want to think about it anymore.

Of course, there are the businesses that supply the quilters and each other. Directly servicing the quilters are the quilt shops and catalog houses. The quilt shops in turn are real, actual brick and mortar as the saying goes and/or virtual and exist in cyber space operating through the unpredictable winds and whims of electrons, programmers and computer manufacturers. And the quilt shops sell a selection of goodies including sewing machines, fabrics, patterns, tools, kits, equipment and supplies of an endless variety; they also provide a diversity of services including teaching, sewing machine repair, color and fabric counseling and so on.

And there are the catalog houses that mail and email catalogs to quilters and most now have web sites to purchase from. As is true with the quilt shops, they handle a wide variety of products and supplies with much of the emphasis on quilt kits and patterns.

Supplying the quilt stores and catalog houses are an endless number and type of large and small manufacturing, computer software, design and distribution firms.

Finally, providing the foundation of the pyramid are the fabric companies that each year vary between setting, estimating or outright missing the trends of the day in styles, colors and materials.

So when someone says, "Oh yea, my grandma used to make quilts. I think I still have one boxed away in the basement or someplace." These are not your grandmother's or even your mother's quilts or quilting processes.

QSH
Keep close track of your needles. Nothing is more disconcerting than stray needles lodged between the sheets.

A Dog's Life

O ur dog, Chutney, a female yellow lab, embodies the epitome of a modern day American pet's life: she is overloved, overprotected, underworked and overfed. Do you detect a note of envy? Not so. If I were to be perfectly honest, and I certainly want to be with my readers, I believe I match up on all those noted criteria pretty well myself. So, no, we are not looking at envy. What we are probably experiencing is a rare moment of self awareness brought about by peering long and hard at someone else.

In any event, Chutney dominates our life, without knowing and without trying. No trip is planned without considering how it will affect her, how will she like/dislike it. So traveling to and participating in a quilt trade show presents special challenges and difficulties.

Prior to a trade show in Portland, Chutney was injured (we never did learn for sure what the cause was). All at once she no longer could place any weight on her left hind leg. Nothing could be more pitiful to the eyes and souls of her guardians, than to watch her hobble on three legs, not whining, complaining or requesting special privileges …well maybe just a little extra food or treats.

Naturally, we had planned to take her to the show with us and had made no provisions for her staying in Helena – nor could we even consider this possibility now – we needed to keep a very close eye on her. So rounds of veterinarian visits, interviews with animal physical therapists, calls to special dog clinics across the country, particularly in Portland, endless hours of Google searches and long telephone conversations with concerned friends and relatives began.

Chutney was examined, tested, prodded, x-rayed, drugged and bandaged and still her left foot remained hovering in the air and we remained in pain and anguish over her plight. She had never before submitted to such infirmity. She lay upon one of her beds and seldom moved, often sighing and sad eyed. Her appetite – which had never been even the slightest affected in the past – noticeably dwindled.

We slept little, worried a lot and accomplished almost nothing as the Trade Show date edged ever closer. Our veterinarian's diagnosis spelled out several possibilities. She certainly had severe arthritis in her joints and particularly the left hock. The hock was very inflamed and swollen and the additional possibility of terminal cancerous tumors was broached. Tests continued, time passed. Finally, one bright light: there was no evidence of cancer. But as the surgical treatment for the problem became clearer, the temporary relief soon vanished. Recommendation: fuse the bones with metal plates by performing a relatively rare operation with a relatively low incidence of success...Great.

For a second opinion, we scheduled a meeting with an animal orthopedic specialist in the Portland area for the day after the show ended. Somehow, we managed to refocus and catch up on most of the things we had let fall behind. We left a day early so that we could take our time driving there and made an untypical overnight stop. The car was packed – the Beverly Hillbillies would have gasped in awe at all we had managed to cram into every corner, every nook and cranny and even the rack on top.

Chutney's left leg was resplendent in a florescent-blue bandage and still waved in the air as she moved about. She was, however, highly reluctant to enter the car when she saw its crowded state. We had fixed a special place for her in one of the back seats, but boxes and a two-wheeled dolly and portions of racks hovered precariously above where her body would be and behind her seat were piles and piles of ...things. I would not have wanted to go either, given these circumstances; in fact, I wasn't too eager to even get behind the steering wheel which was by far a much better locale than the back seat. Ann helped her in as Chutney gave a long groan, raised her eyebrows imploringly, then settled into her seat and in a very few minutes began to snore.

"Well, that's as good a way as any to pass the unpleasant hours ahead," I said stuffing myself behind the wheel. Ann nodded a silent agreement.

The trip seemed to take forever, but at last we arrived in Portland. Fitting our mood, the sky was dreary, a cold rain was falling and I went down a one way street the wrong way. The good news? No one was coming the other way for the short block before our car squealed into the hotel's parking lot.

You'd think being in a reasonably large hotel room, air conditioning on when needed (which we never would have used if it were just us in the room) with the unspoken liberty to crawl up on a huge king sized bed at your leisure with a bowl of cool water and a few nibbles of food within easy reach would not be so bad – particularly in her three legged condition. But we didn't for one second believe Chutney felt that way. No. On the contrary, she was sure, and she made certain we knew she knew, that we were mistreating her in the worst possible way: somehow we were responsible for her dangling leg and then we left her alone for hours on end to a dreary non-existence, without so much as a glimmer of hope of a playful hike in the woods or a comfortable stroll/swim in an icy cold river – in other words, an absolute pit of a life.

The days passed in a predictable, generally grueling fashion: up early, setting up the booth, doing Schoolhouses, taking much welcomed orders and accolades. All in all, a successful show for us, even if it was slightly less well attended than was anticipated by those who predict such events.

During the seemingly endless days, Chutney continued to bravely limp about on three legs with an occasional, semi-cloaked, look of martyrdom. The show seemed to have much less relevance for us than normal as we remained primarily concerned over our ailing pet/daughter. One or two new distributors tracked us down and became new clients; several magazines asked Ann to contribute articles for up-coming issues and new stores became customers...fine – so what about Chutney?

There were many quilt store owners and employees staying at our hotel and they were very gracious as they frequently stopped in our booth to ask how she was doing as they had had glimpses of our walking her, fluorescent bandaged leg hanging, tail wagging an irrepressible hello.

Finally, the trade show ended, we packed up and returned to our hotel room and our dog. Our appointment with the local pet orthopedic specialist was for the following morning and we set our sights on that meeting. We arrived early, waited patiently (kind of) and were eventually shown into the doctor's office. The doctor was dressed all in sickly green that many human and animal doctors seem to prefer these days; a green face mask even hung cosmopolitanly to one side. Light blue eyes sparkled at us beneath a cropping of dark brown hair peeking around his equally rancid-green cotton cap.

X-rays we brought with us were studied; bandages were removed; more x-rays were taken; generic charts showing bones, ligaments and muscles were reviewed. Hushed discussions of a relatively new treatment consisting of stem cell injections and possible bone and tissue rejuvenation were held. All in all, there would be surgery, a recovery period, stem cell injections, therapy, hotel time in a distant city and an undefined success ratio for these types of operations and procedures. The direct cost for the professional services, not counting travel, expenses, possible complications etc. would be in the neighborhood of around $7,500 "... well, might be somewhat higher," he conceded after due reflection.

Despondent and aimless, we decided to turn to one of our favorite pastimes. We had noticed a very large Asian grocery market right around the corner from the doctor's office. I parked and we petted our gloomy dog and went in. We picked silently through the aisles looking for some of our favorite foods. We bought very little.

To ease your concern, in a matter of weeks after our return home, Chutney, sans operations, stem cell injections and surgery, was running around happily on all four legs – almost like new and eating as much (maybe more) than ever, much to our pleasure and to the amazement of the veterinarians.

<u>QSH</u>
Dogs do not mate for life – hence the expression, "You dog".

Food

I've always been amazed to hear people say, "Food doesn't really matter to me," or "He/she is strictly meat and potatoes," or "He/she always eats the same things" etc. Food has been, is and probably will always be a big deal for Ann and me. We delight in the so-called ethnic foods: Indian, Thai, Chinese, Ethiopian, Greek, Mexican, Italian, French and on – all countries, all types. What I have never quite understood is the description of foods as being "Ethnic." Aren't all foods ethnic, including such delights as the ¼ pounder or country fried chicken? No matter, I guess it isn't important how you classify food – you should just enjoy it.

But that's the point of this little chapter, sometimes you really have to work at getting a good meal in the world of quilting.

Firstly, there are the various shows and conventions. Nothing in this world is more dismal than the food served at these places, barring the large group meals served at formal lunch and dinner meetings. And if you are working a booth in a trade show, it's even worse.

Imagine that your world consists of a ten foot by ten foot (we had long ago graduated from a six foot by ten foot booth – no holding us back) area crammed with products and designs for quilt store owners and quilters. Often these booths are manned by one person, at the most two. Of course larger booths have more people, but there are proportionately more products and more demands. How do you find the time to get away to stand in an endless line for your indescribable dish or dry, tasteless sandwich, then nudge into an already crowded table so that you can gulp down the foul tasting morsels which were provided with surly service and at unbelievably high prices? Well often you don't. And, of course, no food is supposed to be consumed in the main convention hall. But Ann had made tasty granola bars and brought small bags of dried fruits and nuts and we scurried and ducked behind piles of quilts to take occasional hurried bites to keep us going.

But all was not totally lost – where there's a will... At the end of the day, we found several good, fun restaurants in all of the different trade show towns...and some great markets for groceries that we could transport back to Montana after the show ended.

One of our favorite dining places was a Greek Restaurant in the Portland area – a historic house converted into an intimate restaurant with approximately 10 tables scattered in several rooms. Decent Greek food: lamb shanks, leg of lamb, Greek salad with feta, stuffed grape leaves, cheese set on fire with blazing streams of brandy, honey, pistachio and phyllo desserts, ouzo to gulp down and cry out "ooopa." And a great ambiance – including dim lights, a cozy fireplace, a gorgeous belly dancer, an elderly accordion player/singer with an unbelievably bad wig, a wisecracking waitress with a thick accent and an owner with a dark blue captain's cap circulating among his guests, trading stories and sharing drinks.

Some of our other highlights were visits to Asian and Italian markets. We love Montana – there is no place we would rather live and we've traveled quite a bit in the United States and abroad. But, Montana does have one major problem as far as we are concerned: the so called ethnic food markets as well as restaurants are basically non-existent. So when we drive to other areas, we swell our already overstuffed van with a myriad of purchases to last us until our next foray. Occasionally, this causes additional problems.

For example, one time we were intent upon stocking up on Asian noodles of all types and so we did. Every crevice, nook and cranny were stuffed with Chinese, Vietnamese and Japanese egg noodles, udon, noodle nests, rice noodles, soba, vermicelli, round spring roll wrappers, rice sticks, thick noodles, thin noodles, average noodles, shrimp flavored noodles, pork flavored noodles, vegetarian noodles and on. It was raining as we crammed the last cellophane package into the last empty spot. Actually, it was pouring – close to a monsoon. But it was a final stop and we were ready to turn towards home, some thousand miles away and it continued to rain as we crossed flooded deserts that never see water, climbed mountain passes that gurgled with ad hoc waterfalls. The gloomy day turned to dark night but we and our noodles forged on.

"You know," I said at the end of a full blast of wind and an extra thick version of downpour, "if the car leaked and the noodles were to become wet, they would expand... and I've been calculating. On the average, noodles expand four times their dry volume when fully saturated with liquid. With the amount of noodles we have stored in the car, their expansion would result in all air being pushed out of the car and, in fact, the noodles would probably smother us before the entire car just exploded from within."

My comment was met with silence. Shortly thereafter, the rain stopped, the car never leaked and we never got the opportunity of determining if my calculations were correct or not.

<u>QSH</u>
"They" say you are getting old if all you ever do at or on a dining room table is eat.

Vacations and Trips

Naturally, a well balanced, healthy life can not be spent solely with quilts and quilt endeavors. I mean life is certainly more than that and vacations, scenic trips, visits to family and friends are an important part of the holistic existence we all anticipate.

Well...in practice, we now take very few vacations or trips and when they do occur, somehow, quilts or quilting are always involved. And here's what really bothers me philosophically: how is it that *The Leader of The Free World* can have about six plus months of vacation a year and the owners of a small pattern design company are at it 24/7 (an expression that I, incidentally, hate)????

Anyway, some examples:

We went camping up in northern Idaho, near the Canadian border – a beautiful camping spot next to a clear, rushing mountain stream – idyllic. On the way home, we planned to stop by several quilt shops to introduce our latest patterns and show samples of the quilts. It was to be a minor interference to our pleasant and long planned few days of pure fun and enjoyment. The back of the van was loaded with plastic bags crammed with quilts and large cartons jammed with patterns. Our camping gear was stuck and sandwiched wherever it could fit, and to get anything out meant moving, removing, positioning and repositioning the quilts and patterns ...all with the greatest of care. It was good that it was a short trip.

Another time found us canoeing and camping overnight on the river – a wonderful, relaxing and nature immersed situation. Except, a great deal of the time was spent with Ann sketching designs on recycled scrap paper for new patterns that the canoeing experience inspired.

Or there was the summer of paranoia when many of the people in our area of Montana were convinced that the huge forest fires that raged all about us would shortly descend upon our homes and bodies with evil abandon. We kept postponing a camping vacation waiting for the fires to diminish. They didn't and we finally decided we would shorten the trip and just go for a few days and closer to home, a river near the border of Wyoming and Montana. And so we packed and left. What we packed was... let's say interesting.

Two huge trunks filled with quilts (honest) and several large cloth bags jammed with design ideas took up most of the space. Next to them I gently placed my lap top computer containing, among other things, all the details of our different patterns. Fortunately, we did manage to shove in some camping gear and supplies.

Once underway, I pursued a point that had been bothering me greatly.

"So, let me understand. It's just possible that a fire may destroy our marvelous home, all our personal and business possessions, our stacks of photo albums and other memorabilia, in short our entire lives, but the idea is that we will be left with trunks of quilts and a computer and the possibility of attending one more Quilt Market and then start our lives anew? Kind of a Phoenix out of the ashes type thing?"

There was no answer forthcoming so I assumed I had made the correct analysis.

But quilts can be quite useful -- don't for a minute think not. And never have they been more useful than when we took a long delayed Christmas trip home to St. Louis to visit relatives and friends.

Of course we brought Christmas gifts; naturally, many of the Christmas gifts were quilts. Requests or hints had come from many of the relatives for lap quilts and Ann had designed them, using minkee as a soft, cuddly, warm backing. She was frantically finishing the gifts as I loaded the car. All was completed except for the binding. Obviously, we needed to take a sewing machine along with everything else so she could finish the binding at her mother's house. The rear of the van was, per usual, packed to the ceiling and I dimly thought of dismantling and throwing out the rear view mirror…who needs to peer into a pile of quilting stuff? Chutney was squeezed in the middle seat once again, huddled among and under bags and boxes.

The trip started out well. The day was sunny and bright and we were making great time as we sped eastward across the long width of Montana. We had just reached the outskirts of Rapid City and were heading towards the Badlands, planning to stop for the night somewhere about half way across South Dakota when the weather started changing. The nice, clear day was disappearing. Still traveling fast, we whizzed by a blinking sign on the highway that we thought said something like "Road closed ahead" – but that wasn't possible. After all, this was Interstate 90 and the day, although no longer sunny, wasn't *that* bad. We kept on. As we continued east, the horizon seemed to blur as the sky and the ground appeared to be merging into one in front of us.

Within ten minutes, all light was gone, thick snow swirled in wild cross drafts of wind, cars threaded in both directions at ten miles per hour. The sides of the road were littered with cars and trucks that had slid off onto the shoulder or into ditches. Sign after sign advertising Wall Drug, the next exit, crept by. It took over three steering-wheel-clutching hours to cover the forty or so miles to Wall. Finally, we were there.

Naturally, there were no vacancies. Most of the larger hotels had closed for the winter and the rest were already packed to the gills. The flashing sign on the highway at this exit (this time, we were going slow enough to read it in its entirety) had clearly said the road was closed from this point on. We discovered that there was temporary shelter being offered at a meeting hall in the center of town and went there to investigate. The hall was almost filled with side by side bodies but there were some blankets and a few spaces on the concrete floor still available. Florescent lights glared overhead and small, energetic children played cowboys/cowgirls and Indians racing amongst the scattered blankets and prostrate people. Chutney could be where? We passed.

We hadn't eaten, knowing a warm, plentiful, country-style meal awaited us when we stopped for the night. Driving around the snow packed streets of Wall showed only one submarine sandwich shop still open. Well, okay, that would be great (hunger has a means of lowering standards). Across the street was a gas station and I decided we had better fill up the tank as the station might be closing. As I hung up the gasoline pump handle, we watched the lights flicker and then go out in the sandwich shop as a neon light stating **Closed** broke the gloom with its pinkish/purplish light. We sighed collectively.

We found a closed motel with a large vacant parking lot and pulled in as far as possible away from the street. Chutney ate. We shared handfuls of homemade granola that Ann had brought as food gifts – so much for the spirit of giving – and washed it down with ice cold red wine.

And it was cold. The last temperature reading we had seen said five degrees and that was several warmer hours ago. It was still snowing as we finished the wine, leaned back in our seats and discussed the logistics of the night ahead. Involuntarily, we stole cold, hard stares at the once again snoring Chutney, envying her comfortable warm bed and the cozy cover we had placed over her.

We sat in the front seats, staring into the darkness and the barely visible wall of the closed motel. We needed to be brave, able to withstand the biting cold that crept through the tiny cracks and seals, that frosted the windows, that ...made it difficult to breathe.

"If we don't make it..." my voice cracked.

"Turn the car and the heater on if you're really cold," Ann said, squeezing her eyes closed as she tugged an extra coat over her chest and lap and snuggled her head further down on the seat.

I also pulled my extra coat around me and attempted to straighten my legs to no avail.

After what seemed a very long while, I said into the stillness, "Blankets would be great."

Ann stirred, muttered, then jolted upright. "We have minkee," she cried.

Following her outburst, she practically leapt out of the car, crunched through the crisp layer of snow around to the back, opened the rear door and tugged at the packages of gift quilts and was back in minutes with several lap sized minkee quilts. In a matter of moments, our bodies were wrapped in furs (albeit fake) and we felt luxuriously warm and safe.

At one of the trade show hotels, I had gotten a black mask to put over my eyes to keep the light out. For some reason, it was still in my coat pocket and I pulled it out and put it in place...in the dark. I also had a black wool stocking cap which I pulled tightly over my ears and made the final clothing adjustment by jamming on my black ski gloves.

Ann was breathing the steady rhythm of a sound sleep, when I knocked soundly on the window and muttered into a make believe walkie talkie in my best southern sheriff drawl, "Lester, come on in... Lester. We got ourselves a situation here. Got a guy with one of those terrorist type stocking caps and a robber's mask that looks like he forgot to cut the eyes out and, well, I think it's some chick cuddled next to him. Looks to me like they must have robbed a furrier someplace. They got damn furs everywhere...don't even have enough money for a hotel room. Furs everywhere – shit. Better send backup."

Ann pushed back the fur, moaned slightly and looked over at me with my black stocking cap pulled over my forehead, my black eye mask and my huge black gloves. She shook her head and then laughed till the tears came. As we were finishing our moment of gaiety, a four wheeler with flashing bright lights and honking warning horns arrived to shovel out the parking lot of the closed-for-the-season motel. It so happened that this was the night of the Winter Solstice, the longest night of the year – talk about timing. In any event, for the remaining hours before dawn, he shoveled and flashed and beeped endlessly while backing. As he left, Ann and I nodded at each other in defeat and then switched places, I started the car and we went in search of breakfast.

But I had learned my lesson: quilts can be helpful – very helpful.

QSH
Keeping a bolt of minkee handy is not a bad idea for some extemporaneous hoohaa.

Quilts and Family

Quilts and family go together like …well, like chocolate and water to steal a title from a great book.

It is the ultimate in family experiences: the pitching in, the joining of kinship, the camaraderie and the accomplishment.

Early in the endeavor of becoming a recognized pattern design company, in addition to creating the design and the quilt, marketing the new design and preparing the instructions, patterns and diagrams, we also printed, collated, folded and stuffed the patterns into 6" x 9" shiny plastic bags (shiny, very slippery plastic bags, I must add).

One exciting day, we received our largest order to date – I think it was 288 each of two patterns. We felt we had to ship them within two days after receipt of the order (didn't want to ask the buyer how long would be okay) and were totally panicked.

Ann's sister, let's call her "Sister Sue", was visiting us and offered help and a suggestion.

"Let's have a stuffing party," she said – a stroke of genius I thought.

So we did. We invited Ann's cousins, let's call them, "The Cousins – Win and Al," who live in Helena, were instrumental in our moving there and were more helpful than anyone could ever be at every stage of our new lives. Well, you know that old Chinese proverb, "Save a person's life and they are your obligation for life"...or something like that.

Call us deceitful? Perhaps. We touted the stuffing party as an especially interesting menu of crab stuffed mushrooms, fruit stuffed pork loin and couscous stuffed tomatoes plus a just plain stuffing dessert. We did barely mention the possibility that there might be some slight amount of assistance involved in helping us get out a very large order and it might be a good idea to arrive three to four hours before dinner. They did so with good will and no stuffing pulled over their eyes and we all sat down and stuffed. Around six hundred patterns is a lot of patterns to collate, fold and stuff and dinner was even later than normal.

The following week we met with a local printer and henceforth stuffed no more.

Another time, Sister Sue was planning to visit us and for fun and, hopefully profit, we all decided to have a *Two Sister's Sale* at our home.

Sister Sue, among other things, is a very talented weaver and creates, designs, dyes and markets her own line of fashionable wearable art. She markets at elite art shows around the country and had just completed one in San Francisco. Instead of shipping her inventory back to her home outside of Columbia, Missouri, she shipped it to our home in Montana; she would bring any additional items needed such as mannequins, racks etc. in her car when she drove to Helena. Ann did a great job of marketing with the local newspaper which agreed to do a write up including pictures in their weekly "What's going on around town" insert for several weeks prior to the sale.

Sister Sue's inventory arrived. Then Sister Sue (and two faithful dogs) arrived, van loaded to the top as seems to be a family trait. Ann gathered her quilts from closets and trunks. The Sale was to be held as a three day open house, Saturday, Sunday and Monday (for those who might have been off enjoying the Big Sky outdoors over the weekend). Saturday was two days away and all had to be made ready for turning the house into a virtual gallery of sisterly fine art.

Hour after hour passed until quilts hung from every wall, were draped and stacked over couches and beds and flowed down quilt ladders. Our bedroom had become a rack filled fiesta of gorgeous colors of hand-woven jackets, shirts, coats and vests. Mannequins dressed to kill whispered to each other in corners throughout the house and snuggled chummily on the staircase leading to the loft. By ten Friday night, we felt we were prepared for the crowds that would be coming the next several days.

Build a house of quilts and wearable art and they will come. And come they did. We had set the opening to begin at what we thought was a respectable hour, 9 a.m. A group of overeager ladies rang the bell at 7:45. For three solid days, happy, smiling women (with an occasional ill-at-ease man in tow) strolled from room to room through our home, complimenting the two sisters on the uniqueness and beauty of their work and suggesting that this should be a yearly event. For three solid days, we had nowhere we could live or even sit: chairs, beds, and couches were laden with merchandise. Even the kitchen and deck were in constant use as we provided ice tea and home made pastries for the enthused ladies and handcuffed spouses.

Finally it was Monday evening. It was over. Some quilts had been sold; some woven wearable art had been sold. We gulped down drinks, discussed the sale and unanimously agreed, "Never again." After all, it is our home, not a shop.

Ann also has cousins in Houston, call them Tom and Majel, and they have been kind enough to assist us each time we have attended the Fall International Trade Show in Houston.

Their assistance included our staying in their home the night before the show started and the night after it ended plus pick ups and drops offs at the airport and hotel plus – and if you ever heard of a BIG plus, this is it – helping us set up and take down our booth. Now Tom is six foot eight which totally eliminated any need for ladders or step stools, and Majel is a bundle of helpful nervous energy and a terrific detail person. Hey, what are families for?

QSH
Having family participation is not necessarily incest.

You Wanted to Write?

From my youth, I had always expected to be a writer. Short stories, poems and essays flew off my pen or pencil in my teens and early 20s. Then, as the cliché goes, life got in the way or, more correctly, I allowed life to get in the way. With the speed of light, decades passed and I had almost ceased writing when I suddenly became determined that this would not happen. So I decided to write novels and have now completed two of them and even plan to properly market them someday. But other opportunities came my way.

I now write most of the copy on our quilt patterns. For example, one of the patterns is called *Gathering Storm* which is an amazingly artistic and realistic pictorial of a gorgeous horse racing ahead of an oncoming storm. So the back cover states, "Clouds darken; lightning flashes; the wind whirls and the sleek mare searches for safety." One more example of my new writing career is found on our nine patch, quilt-as-you-go pattern, *Stripped to the Nines*. The cover says, "You've been dressed to the nines – now you can be stripped to the nines. Happy stripping."

Is that writing or what?

Novel writing and its subsequent marketing has always been tough, but today, it is harder then ever. The consolidation of the publishing houses and the rising importance of the big box book stores...and, yes, *Walmart*, have completely changed the system of manuscript reviews and acceptance, book publishing and distribution. Always a big help, literary agents are now a necessity. It is almost impossible for an unpublished author to have direct correspondence with editors of publishing houses. And to make it all the worse, literary agents are overloaded with seemingly endless queries by would-be writers.

In between the inspirations of sentences on pattern covers, I'm working on marketing my finished works and planning my third novel. (And I even managed to sneak in this short account. Of course I entered into the writing of this book aware that I was doing so at great personal risk – as is true for any person who courageously speaks out and exposes a vile system of any kind.)

Who knows, someday, someone may even get the chance to read one of them.

And of course, there are always magazines. There is a line that has stuck in my mind for many years from, I believe, one of Tennessee Williams' plays. Truthfully I can't recall which one, but a woman, defending her degree of intelligence and literacy, says in a heavy drawl something like, "Well, I am a magazine reader."

And now I too am a magazine reader (on a very limited basis) – well ever since Ann became published in several quilt magazines.

As with all facets of life, achieving something or even attempting to achieve something is seldom easy.

Our continually helpful friend, Jackie, suggested that Ann might do well to try to get articles/patterns published in some of the larger magazines and then took the next step of actually introducing her to several women who were with these publishers. A great start.

The trials and tribulations of getting published in a magazine represent events that are a microcosm of the very paths of our existence: there is the introduction, the learning of requirements, the defining of rules and the submission of works and accomplishments, all occurring at a snail's pace. Then suddenly, there is acceptance and demand, all occurring just under the speed of light. Meet it or miss it.

A typical situation was as follows.

It's late summer, time to prepare for the fall trade show, creating the quilts that were only vague ideas rummaging along in the back of your mind, choosing the perfect fabrics and colors, writing the detailed instructions, testing the patterns, preparing marketing materials and all the general tasks required for the fall market itself – not to mention the day to day operation of our business. The phone rings.

It's an editor from a major magazine.

"Hi, Ann. Like to have you do a nice little article for us on *whatever.* Are you interested?"

"Sure."

"Great, just need a few things to start."

"Swell."

"Well, would like to get sketches of a new quilt design regarding the *whatever* along with a summary write up."

"Okay…" There was now a note of hesitancy in Ann's voice. "When will you need it?"

"We have some time on this phase; the week after next will work fine."

"The week after next?"

"Yes, and we wouldn't need the finished quilt and detailed instructions for another two to three weeks after that."

"This is the time we get ready for market, you know?"

A warm, condescending laugh followed by, "Oh, yes, I know, but I also know this will not be a big deal for you… and the coverage will be great."

And so it starts.

Anyway to date Ann has been published in a variety of national quilt magazines and even has one outstanding article in a magazine in Great Britain.

Well, at least one of us is published.

<u>QSH</u>
Book IS a four letter word.

So Where was the Sex?

W e're at the end and some of you may be asking, "So where was the sex you alluded to anyway?"

Perhaps there has been less explicitness than you might have anticipated given my original title. But, look, quilters have imagination. Use yours. And think of this, if there's no money (and trust me, there isn't), and no glory, what else could there be that would induce someone like me to continue? Just answer me that.

QSH
Last Hint: Could it be love?

Some Background Information

The Author (abused spouse): Norb had been an aspiring writer for many years, but had confused aspiring with perspiring and, consequently, had avoided the same. One night his wife explained the difference and he immediately became inspired to aspire once again.

Norb holds an MBA from Stanford University and has held top level executive positions with large corporations but has primarily owned and operated several medium sized businesses. **Norb@GrizzlyGulchGallery.com**

Ann Lauer (abusing spouse): Ann is a fiber artist who has been involved with quilting for over 20 years. In late 2005, she founded a quilt pattern business, Grizzly Gulch Gallery. In addition to designing patterns, she teaches and creates custom quilts. **Ann@ GrizzlyGulchGallery.com**

Grizzly Gulch Gallery is located in the mountains above Helena, Montana in an area known as Grizzly Gulch. The website is **www. GrizzlyGulchGalley.com** for retail customers and **www.GrizzlyGulchWholesale.com** for quilt shops.

LaVergne, TN USA
07 October 2009
160113LV00001B/4/P